The Mexican War

by Marc Tyler Nobleman

Content Adviser: Dr. Armando Cantú Alonzo, Associate Professor,
Department of History, Texas A & M University

Reading Adviser: Rosemary G. Palmer, Ph.D., Department of Literacy,
College of Education, Boise State University

COMPASS POINT BOOKS
MINNEAPOLIS, MINNESOTA

Compass Point Books
3109 West 50th Street, #115
Minneapolis, MN 55410

Visit Compass Point Books on the Internet at *www.compasspointbooks.com*
or e-mail your request to *custserv@compasspointbooks.com*

On the cover: The storming of Chapultepec on September 13, 1847

Photographs ©: Library of Congress, cover, 5, 14, 15, 21, 31; North Wind Picture Archives, 4, 8, 12, 17, 20, 23, 30; Special Collections Division/University of Texas at Arlington Libraries, 6, 37; Chicago Historical Society, 7; MPI/Getty Images, 9; Bettmann/Corbis, 10, 32; Courtesy Ronald Cramer, 18; Lombard Antiquarian Maps & Prints, 19, 29; Courtesy of Army Art Collection, U.S. Army Center of Military History, 22; DVIC/NARA, 25; Stock Montage, 27, 29; Courtesy of the National Museum of the U.S. Army, Army Art Collection, 34; The Newberry Library/Stock Montage, 35, 36; Corbis, 38; Adam Woolfitt/Corbis.

Creative Director: Terri Foley
Managing Editor: Catherine Neitge
Editor: Jennifer VanVoorst
Photo Researcher: Svetlana Zhurkina
Designer/Page production: Bradfordesign, Inc./Les Tranby
Cartographer: XNR Productions, Inc.
Educational Consultant: Diane Smolinski

Library of Congress Cataloging-in-Publication Data
Nobleman, Marc Tyler.
  The Mexican War / by Marc Tyler Nobleman.
    p. cm. — (We the people)
Includes bibliographical references (p.   ) and index.
  ISBN 0-7565-0841-X
  1. Mexican War, 1846-1848—Juvenile literature. I. Title. II. We the people (Series)
  (Compass Point Books)
    E404.N63 2004
    973.6'2—dc22   2004016343

TABLE OF CONTENTS

ARMY AT THE GATES

The year was 1847. U.S. General Winfield Scott and his troops were far from home. For six months, they had marched from the eastern coast of Mexico toward Mexico City, the country's capital, fighting Mexican soldiers and

The U.S. Army approaches Mexico City in the final stages of the Mexican War.

citizens along the way. The journey had been hot and exhausting for the U.S. soldiers, as well as for the Mexicans they confronted. The two countries had been at war for a year and a half, and some of the men sensed that the end—whatever it might be—was approaching.

American General Winfield Scott

Scott paused at the gates of Mexico City. U.S. President James K. Polk had ordered him to offer Mexico one last chance to agree to American terms of peace. If the Mexicans agreed, their city could be spared. If not, Scott's army would storm Mexico City with cannons, rifles, and bayonets.

When the Mexican government refused to discuss America's offer, Scott did not hesitate. He ordered his men to move in. The capital of Mexico was under siege.

A WAR BETWEEN NEIGHBORS

In the Revolutionary War (1775–1783), the 13 American colonies fought with their founding country, Great Britain. In the American Civil War (1861–1865), the United States fought with itself, the North versus the South. In between these famous wars, though—from 1846 to 1848—the United States fought with its neighboring country, Mexico.

In the United States, this war is known as the Mexican War or the Mexican-American War. In Mexico, some people refer to it as *Guerra de Estados Unidos con Mexico* ("War of the United States

This 1847 political cartoon shows U.S. President Polk preparing to take his slice of Mexico's territorial pie.

Against Mexico"). The fact that they do not call it "War of the United States *and* Mexico" suggests that the Mexican people did not feel that both sides entered the conflict with equal desire.

According to many Mexicans, the United States invaded Mexico, not the other way around, as some Americans believe. That is why another Mexican name for the war translates as "The U.S. Invasion." Regardless of what it is called, this war had a deep and lasting effect on each country.

This poster illustrates major figures and battles of the Mexican War.

FROM INDEPENDENCE TO WAR

Throughout history, war has often led to independence. However, in the Mexican War, independence led to war.

In the early 1800s, the land we now call Texas was a part of Mexico. However, by 1834, more than 30,000 U.S. settlers lived in Texas, as opposed to only 7,500 Mexican-born people. In 1836, Texas declared itself an independent republic. Many Mexicans felt betrayed by Texas' declaration and could not accept Texas as an independent nation. Though other countries— including the United

In 1836, American forces fought Mexican troops at the Alamo. It was the first battle fought after Texas declared its independence from Mexico.

8

Austin was named capital of the Republic of Texas.

States, Great Britain, and France—did recognize Texas as its own nation, most Mexicans felt that Texas was Mexican territory that had temporarily been taken over by rebels.

In 1845, nine years after declaring independence from Mexico, Texas citizens voted to join the United States. On December 29, 1845, the United States annexed Texas as the 28th state. Many Mexicans considered the annexation an act of war because they still believed Texas was rightfully theirs. In addition, Mexico soon learned that the United States was after more Mexican territory—much more—and that it would go to great lengths to get it.

On February 19, 1846, Texas celebrated officially becoming a state.

OTHER CAUSES OF WAR

The United States' annexation of Texas was only one cause of the Mexican War. Another cause was disagreement between Mexico and the United States over the location of the border between the two countries. When Texas was part of Mexico, that border was the Nueces River. However, the United States now claimed that Texas extended 160 miles (257 kilometers) south of that river to another river, the Rio Grande. That meant the territory between those two rivers would be part of Texas, not Mexico. Mexicans did not agree with this new boundary.

Still another issue that prompted war involved compensation. After Mexico itself became independent from Spain in 1821, the country tried several times to establish a system of government. Many Mexican citizens, however, were unsatisfied and revolted frequently. Some U.S. citizens were injured or had their property damaged in these revolts. They wanted Mexico to pay them for their injuries or losses. Mexico could not afford to do that and did not believe that doing so was its responsibility.

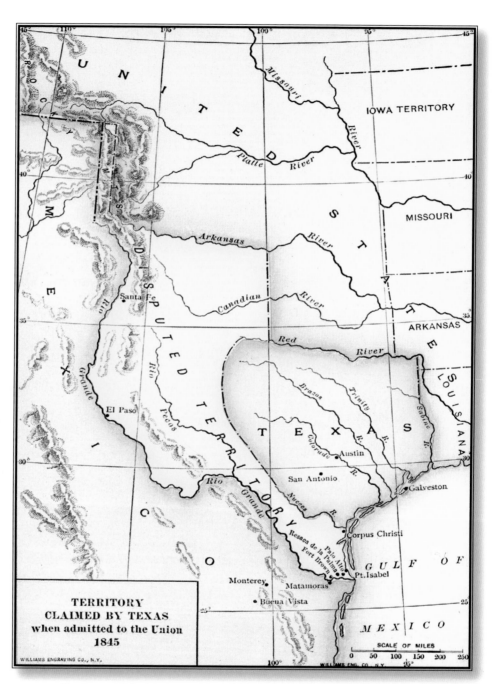

TERRITORY
CLAIMED BY TEXAS
when admitted to the Union
1845

WILLIAMS ENGRAVING CO., N.Y.

SCALE OF MILES
0   50   100   150   200   250

WILLIAMS ENG. CO., N.Y.

12   *One cause of the Mexican War was a disagreement over Mexico's border with Texas.*

A final cause of the Mexican War involved the land that is now the state of California. This land—and much of what is now the southwestern United States—was a part of Mexico at that time. Many Americans had settled in Mexican territories, including California. If this land were to become part of the United States, then the nation would stretch across the entire North American continent and have ports on the Pacific Ocean.

Although some modern historians compare the United States' actions at this time to that of a bully picking on a smaller, weaker country, many Americans in the 1800s did not see it that way. The idea of Manifest Destiny was popular with Americans at the time. Manifest Destiny was a belief that Americans had the right to expand the boundaries of their country. Americans felt they had this right because they believed their democratic government was better than other governments. By taking more land, they were helping others by spreading democracy. Of course, none of this benefited Mexico, which intended to keep California, the land south of the Nueces River, and other lands in the Southwest that the United States wanted.

This painting shows Americans heading west guided by a woman in white, a symbol of Manifest Destiny.

14

AN ATTEMPT AT A SETTLEMENT

President James K. Polk

After the United States annexed Texas as a state, relations between the two countries began to break down. To keep them from getting any worse, U.S. President James K. Polk sent diplomat John Slidell to Mexico City. When Slidell arrived in December 1845, Mexico's political situation was a mess. Revolts by Mexicans unhappy with their government were still tearing the country apart, and the government was not stable.

Slidell's mission was to resolve the issues between Mexico and the United States. He offered a deal: the United States would not push Mexico to pay for the American losses

15

due to Mexican uprisings if Mexico accepted the Rio Grande as the boundary between Mexico and Texas. He also offered to buy Mexican land that is now California and New Mexico for as much as $30 million.

Mexican officials were furious. They did not want to make any deals with the United States, and they did not want to give up any more territory, even for such a price. Mexican president José Joaquín de Herrera refused to meet with Slidell. Only weeks later, Mariano Paredes overthrew Herrera and became Mexico's new president. Paredes did not like the United States and was willing to go to war rather than give in to American demands.

Tension built not only between the two countries, but within them as well. Some Americans wanted a war, particularly those citizens who supported slavery. In the United States, each state was either a slave state or a free state, meaning they either allowed or did not allow slavery. People in slave states wanted more slave-holding territory, but people in free states did not want Texas—or any other

Slavery was legal in the Southern states.

area that the U.S. might acquire—to become a slave state.
Despite their differing ideas, volunteers from both slave and
free states signed up to serve in the military, even from areas
that had not yet become states, such as what is now
California and Iowa.

The Mexican people were also divided about war.
Some admired the United States for providing many
opportunities for wealth and supported the country's
ambitions. Others feared the U.S. and felt threatened as it
became a powerful country.

17

U.S. soldier Washington Cramer's enlistment paper to fight in the Mexican War.

THE WAR BEGINS

Fearing a Mexican attack on the disputed Texas land, U.S. President Polk sent troops to the Rio Grande in the summer of 1845. These troops were under the command of General Zachary Taylor. Taylor did not resemble the typical general of the day. He preferred to wear a straw hat with his uniform, and some

U.S. General Zachary Taylor

thought he looked more like a farmer than a soldier. Nevertheless, Taylor was an able leader who was respected for his courage and popular with his men. His nickname was "Old Rough and Ready."

Taylor and his soldiers did not go to the border to start a war. They went to defend the United States in case

Mexico did. Mexican troops were stationed on the other side of the river, on the southern bank of the Rio Grande.

On April 25, 1846, however, war became a reality. At the direction of General Mariano Arista, about 2,000 Mexican soldiers crossed the Rio Grande and surprised a group of fewer than 100 U.S. soldiers. The Mexicans killed 11 Americans and took most of the rest prisoner. To Mexico, the United States had caused the hostilities by occupying Mexican territory. To the U.S., however, Mexico was at fault by refusing to make a deal and by firing the first shots.

U.S. forces under General Zachary Taylor camped across the Rio Grande from the Mexican troops.

By the time President Polk learned of this incident, Mexicans and Americans had already fought two more battles in Texas. The battle at Palo Alto on May 8 and at

General Zachary Taylor led U.S. forces to victory in the Battle of Palo Alto.

Resaca de la Palma the following day were both American victories. The president told Congress that "Mexico has … invaded our territory and shed American blood upon the American soil." In reality, of course, this territory was in dispute, and Mexico could make the same claim to the land.

Nevertheless, on May 13, 1846, the United States declared war on Mexico. While Mexico did not formally declare war in return, it did not plan to let the United States have its way and take what it believed to be Mexican land.

21

WAR IN THE SOUTH

The Mexican War took place in three main regions at the same time: Mexico, today's American Southwest, and the area that is now California. Despite Mexico's defeats at Palo Alto and Resàca de la Palma, the Mexican government thought they would win in the end. The U.S. soldiers would be fighting on foreign ground. In war, being unfamiliar with the land can be a disadvantage. In addition, the Mexican army was larger than the U.S. Army, and it also had recent combat experience in the numerous Mexican rebellions.

Many soldiers joined the U.S. Army seeking adventure.

22

Mexican officers who fought in the Mexican War were likely to be wealthy landowners.

After the early American victories, however, more men joined the U.S. Army, and with each passing week, the numbers grew. Although some of the American soldiers had trained at the U.S. Military Academy in West Point, New York, most were volunteers in their late teens and early 20s. Few of these young men had ever been away from home. On the Mexican side, the average soldier, or *soldado*, was a peasant who owned no land, while their officers were often wealthy landowners. Though soldiers on both sides signed up for adventure and glory, the reality of war was very different. Instead, they faced long, hot marches, boredom, illness, injuries, or death.

General Taylor and his troops entered Mexico, moving slowly at first. The summer of 1846 was very hot, and most of the Americans were not used to a subtropical climate. Their camps were dirty, and diseases spread quickly. Luckily for them, the Mexicans did not attack. The Mexican government was still not stable.

American troops attack the Bishop's Palace in the Battle of Monterrey.

President Paredes left office. Over the next few months, the leadership of the Mexican government changed several times.

On September 21, 1846, Taylor's troops began fighting Mexicans in the Battle of Monterrey, in northern Mexico. The clash was brutal, with some men engaging in hand-to-hand combat in the streets. On September 24, after five hard days of fighting, the Americans captured the city of Monterrey.

WAR IN THE WEST

While General Taylor's troops moved south through Mexico, troops under General Stephen Kearny were moving west. On August 18, 1846, Kearny's forces took over the town of Santa Fe, in what is now the state of New Mexico. Mexican merchants and traders in Santa Fe were already involved in peaceful trade with Americans, which they wanted to maintain. They gave little resistance. The takeover was done without bloodshed.

Moving into California, Kearny found that Americans already controlled a portion of the Mexican province. Settlers there were interested in becoming part of the United States. Like the people in New Mexico, they liked the American promise of freedom and opportunity. Some had previously revolted against Mexican authorities.

General Stephen Kearny takes over Santa Fe, New Mexico.

Kearny, along with Commodore John Sloat, Commodore Robert Stockton, and Lieutenant Colonel John Frémont, finished the conquest of California—first in the upper part of the future state, then the lower. On January 13, 1847, the Treaty of Cahuenga was signed near Los Angeles, ending the fighting in California.

Lieutenant Colonel John Frémont and California settlers declare their independence from Mexico.

SANTA ANNA

The Americans' winning streak continued in the south with several battle victories in early 1847. On February 22 and 23, Taylor fought what would be his most important conflict in the Mexican War, the Battle of Buena Vista. The Mexican troops were led by General Antonio López de Santa Anna, who was also acting president of Mexico.

Mexican General Antonio López de Santa Anna

Santa Anna was a wealthy, intelligent man who loved his country. In fact, he had already been Mexico's president twice before. He had an arrogant personality and liked to be in the spotlight. He was not gifted at military strategy, but he knew how to deal with other people. He was usually good at turning things in his favor.

29

The Battle of Buena Vista, however, did not go his way. Although the Mexican army numbered around 20,000 soldiers and the Americans numbered only 5,000, it was an especially difficult battle—the bloodiest in the Mexican War. Some estimate that nearly 3,500 Mexicans were killed, wounded, or went missing. American losses were counted at 1,500 or fewer. In the end, though, Santa Anna's forces withdrew, earning Taylor a major victory and marking the end of armed conflict in northern Mexico.

Mexican soldiers charge U.S. forces at Buena Vista.

TARGET: MEXICO CITY

President Polk knew that to win the war, the U.S. Army had to take Mexico's capital. After the Battle of Buena Vista, Polk set his sights on Mexico City. For that task, he relied on General Winfield Scott, at that time the highest-ranking officer in the U.S. Army.

U.S. General Winfield Scott

Scott was often arrogant, but he had a brilliant sense of military strategy. He followed rules precisely, and, unlike General Taylor, he was formal in his military dress and behavior. His nickname was "Old Fuss and Feathers."

31

As General Scott and his army of about 12,000 traveled by sea to Mexico, the Mexicans braced for another invasion. In March 1847, Scott landed close to Veracruz, Mexico's most important seaport on the Gulf of Mexico. After a siege lasting almost three weeks, Scott and his troops took Veracruz.

After a long siege, U.S. General Winfield Scott landed his troops at Veracruz.

The 8,500 soldiers then began the 300-mile (500-km) trek inland across mountains and through mud toward Mexico City and the final campaign of the war. En route, they met Santa Anna's army at the mountain pass of Cerro Gordo. There, the U.S. Army surprised the Mexicans by attacking from several directions, pulling their cannons and supplies up the hills with rope.

The Americans defeated Santa Anna's troops and moved on to other victories with the battles of Contreras and Churubusco in August. Though the Mexican armies regularly outnumbered Scott's army, Mexico was undergoing so much strife that its armies could not unite to stop the American advance.

On August 22, 1847, General Scott offered the Mexicans an armistice so the two sides could try to settle their differences. After two weeks of discussion, though, they could not agree on terms for peace. On September 8, fighting resumed just outside Mexico City.

The U.S. Army won another victory in the Battle of Churubusco.

The Mexicans fiercely defended their capital. On September 13, they fought with Americans at Chapultepec, a great fortress on a hill overlooking the city. At the time, the fortress was being used as a military academy, and many of the teenage cadets chose to join the 8,000-man defense force. The Mexicans were defeated, and the last six teenage soldiers chose to die rather than surrender. According to legend, one of them wrapped himself in the Mexican flag and jumped off the fortress wall to his death.

On September 14, Scott led his army into Mexico City. A small group of U.S. soldiers raised the American

American forces stormed the Mexican fortress Chapultepec in one of the last battles of the Mexican War.

Having taken the fortress of Chapultepec, General Scott led his troops into Mexico City.

flag at the National Palace, which was called the Halls of the Montezumas.

Though both sides had suffered terrible losses, Scott's six-month effort paid off. Santa Anna evacuated his troops, and on September 16, he resigned from the presidency. Soon after, he resigned from his military position, too. With the fall of Mexico City, the fighting, for the most part, was over.

36

PEACE AND REMEMBRANCE

The new Mexican president, Pedro Maria Anaya, and American peace commissioner Nicholas Trist began to discuss a peace treaty in November 1847. The Treaty of Guadalupe Hidalgo was signed on February 2, 1848, officially ending the Mexican War.

The treaty

The Treaty of Peace, Friendship, Limits, and Settlement was signed by the United States and Mexico in November 1847.

settled the Texas boundary dispute by designating the Rio Grande as its southern border. Mexico surrendered almost half of its territory to the United States, including part or all of the present states of Texas, California, Colorado,

Utah, Nevada, Arizona, and New Mexico. The surrendered land covered 525,000 square miles (1,360,000 square kilometers).

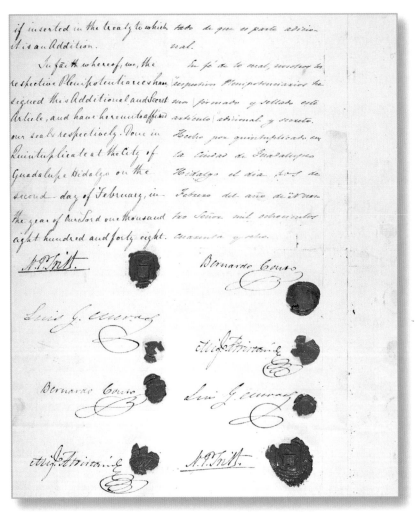

Mexican and U.S. representatives signed and sealed the Treaty of Guadalupe Hidalgo.

Though much of the land had not been heavily populated or controlled by Mexicans, it was a massive loss to Mexico. In exchange, the United States paid Mexico $15 million for the land and agreed to handle the claims of Americans who felt they were owed money by Mexico.

Victory often comes with tragedy. Approximately 5,800 Americans were killed or wounded in combat. In addition to the loss of territory, Mexico lost around 13,000 soldiers in combat, and 1,300 more were wounded. Thousands more soldiers on both sides died from disease.

The war cost the United States an estimated $75 million. It also continued the debate between those who opposed slavery and those who favored it. Should this newly acquired land become slave-holding territory or free territory? No one knew it yet, but these disagreements would lead to the American Civil War.

The war cost Mexico more than money. Its government and economy were in shambles, and many cities, roads, and homes were destroyed. With so much Mexican

In Texas, the Rio Grande marks the border between the United States and Mexico.

land now part of the United States, some families were even split up, with members living in different countries. Many Mexicans felt humiliated by their country's loss. As was happening in the United States, problems arising from the Mexican War would later lead to a Mexican Civil War.

Today, Mexico and the United States are good neighbors. The countries are on good terms, and each is proud of its own history. The sting of the war between them may have faded, but the brave actions of soldiers on both sides will always be remembered.

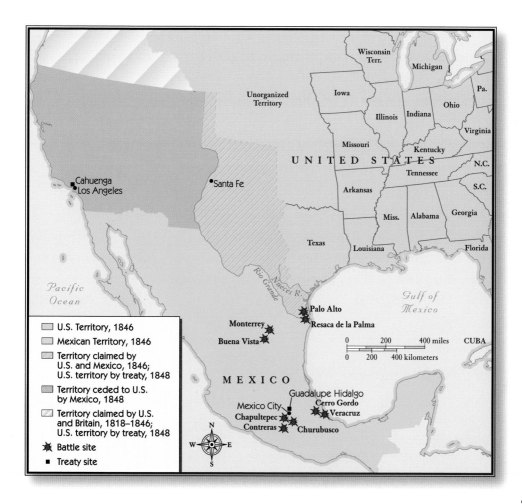

GLOSSARY

annexed—taken and added to the territory of a country

armistice—an agreement between opponents at war to stop fighting and discuss peace

campaign—an organized effort of a war

compensation—payment made to cover a loss or injury

province—a district or region of some countries

republic—a form of government in which the people elect representatives to manage the government

siege—a military action in which one side surrounds an enemy position for a long time to cut off supplies and force a surrender

uprisings—conflicts against a ruling power

DID YOU KNOW?

- In 1848, the same year the Mexican War ended, General Zachary Taylor was elected the 12th president of the United States. Ulysses S. Grant, the 18th president of the United States, also served in the Mexican War.

- The Mexican War was a war of firsts: It was the first war the United States fought on foreign soil, the first war anywhere in the world to be photographed, and the first war in which newspaper journalists reported from within war zones.

- In the "Marines' Hymn," the opening phrase, "From the Halls of Montezuma," refers to the Mexican War, where the U.S. soldiers raised an American flag outside the National Palace, or the Halls of the Montezumas, in Mexico City.

- Some American soldiers switched sides and fought for Mexico. One such group of soldiers was the San Patricios, or Saint Patrick's Battalion. Most were Irish-born Americans who felt the United States was cruel to Mexico and felt allegiance to Mexico because of their shared Catholic faith. The San Patricios are remembered as heroes in Mexico.

IMPORTANT DATES

Timeline

1810	Mexico declares itself independent from Spain.
1821	Mexico becomes a free country after 11 years of war with Spain.
1836	Texas, formerly a part of Mexico, declares itself an independent republic.
1845	The United States annexes Texas as the 28th state, angering Mexico; President James K. Polk sends John Slidell to Mexico to negotiate peace.
1846	President James K. Polk declares war on Mexico; the United States takes over New Mexico and California; General Zachary Taylor's troops defeat Mexican troops in the Battle of Monterrey.
1847	General Taylor defeats General Antonio López de Santa Anna in the Battle of Buena Vista; General Winfield Scott conquers Mexico City.
1848	The Treaty of Guadalupe Hidalgo is signed, ending the Mexican War.

IMPORTANT PEOPLE

MARIANO ARISTA (1802–1855)
Mexican general who led troops in the earliest battles of the Mexican War

MARIANO PAREDES (1797–1849)
President of Mexico when the Mexican War started

JAMES K. POLK (1795–1849)
11th president of the United States who led the United States into the Mexican War

ANTONIO LÓPEZ DE SANTA ANNA (1794–1876)
President of Mexico and a general who led the Mexican armies in the Mexican War

WINFIELD SCOTT (1786–1866)
American general who conquered Mexico City in the Mexican War

ZACHARY TAYLOR (1784–1850)
American general who won several key northern battles in the Mexican War; he was elected the 12th president of the United States in 1848.

WANT TO KNOW MORE?

At the Library

Carey, Charles W. *The Mexican War: Mr. Polk's War.* Berkeley Heights, N.J.: Enslow Publishers, 2002.

Mills, Bronwyn. *U.S.-Mexican War.* New York: Facts on File, 2003.

Nardo, Don. *The Mexican-American War.* San Diego: Lucent Books, 1999.

O'Connell, Kim A. *The Mexican-American War.* Berkeley Heights, N.J.: Enslow Publishers, 2003.

On the Web

For more information on *The Mexican War,* use FactHound
to track down Web sites related to this book.

1. Go to *www.facthound.com*
2. Type in a search word related to this book
   or this book ID: 075650841X.

3. Click on the *Fetch It* button.

Your trusty FactHound will fetch the best Web sites for you!

On the Road

Fort Scott National Historic Site

P.O. Box 918

Fort Scott, KS

620/223-0310

To see a historic fort from the time of the Mexican War; soldiers from Fort Scott served under General Zachary Taylor in the Mexican War

Palo Alto Battlefield National Historic Site

1623 Central Blvd., #213

Brownsville, TX 78520

956/541-2785

To visit the only Mexican War battlefield in the U.S. National Parks system

Look for more We the People books about this era:

The Alamo

The Arapaho and Their History

The Battle of the Little Bighorn

The Buffalo Soldiers

The California Gold Rush

The Chumash and Their History

The Creek and Their History

The Erie Canal

Great Women of the Old West

The Lewis and Clark Expedition

The Louisiana Purchase

The Ojibwe and Their History

The Oregon Trail

The Pony Express

The Powhatan and Their History

The Santa Fe Trail

The Transcontinental Railroad

The Trail of Tears

The Wampanoag and Their History

The War of 1812

A complete list of We the People titles is available on our Web site:
www.compasspointbooks.com

INDEX

About the Author

Marc Tyler Nobleman has written more than 40 books for young readers. He has written for a History Channel show called The Great American History Quiz and for children's magazines, including *Nickelodeon, Highlights for Children,* and *Read* (a *Weekly Reader* publication). He is also a cartoonist whose single panels have appeared in more than 100 magazines internationally. He lives with his wife and daughter in Connecticut.